SEED CELESTIAL

SEED CELESTIAL

WINNER OF THE AUTUMN HOUSE POETRY PRIZE

SARA R. BURNETT

AUTUMN
HOUSE PRESS

Pittsburgh, PA

This project is supported in part by an award from the National Endowment for the Arts. To find out more about how National Endowment for the Arts grants impact individuals and communities, visit www.arts.gov.

Autumn House Press receives state arts funding support through a grant from the Pennsylvania Council on the Arts, a state agency funded by the Commonwealth of Pennsylvania, and the National Endowment for the Arts, a federal agency.

cover art: Art by Dorothy Lathrop for *Down-Adown-Derry* by Walter de la Mare (1922)
book design: Tyler Crumrine

ISBN: 978-1-63768-052-0
Library of Congress Control Number: 2022938580

for Colin, my husband,
for Maia & Aidan, my children,
y para mis abuelos

CONTENTS

I. SEED

II. ANIMAL

III. WORD

IV. EARTH

V. CELESTIAL

Notes
Acknowledgments

I. SEED

Every thing created needs a seed from which to cast
Into the gentle breezes of the air.
— Lucretius, I. 205-6

Ab Ovo

(from Latin meaning "from the beginning" or "from the egg")

so not from nothing, my yolk
      and hatchling, pomegranate jewel
            set in membrane, clot and thread,

honey of the hive. I didn't know you,
      one of seven million chances
            hibernating in a fluid sac

waiting for the signal to implant
      yourself. Out of the vestibular bulb,
            the tulip, the peacock feather,

the fern. In another life, you were a crocus
      pushing up through snow. I was a doe
            crossing a busy stretch of road

alone. Unfurl your leaves, your top-heavy
      camellia head. You made a bed
            from pressed petals

in the swaddling dark. Your body was
      that supple. I kept a wad of soaked
            cabbage leaves to cool the sores.

Forgive the ways I'm ill-prepared
      to receive you, for you to break
            from this body

into your own. In another life, I was the wind
      prickling your ear to keep you still.
            You were a deer in tall grass.

Theory of Probability I

If the refrigerator hadn't broken
if the train had come on time

if it had been snowing harder
and slick ice paved the black lacquered road

if the loud, drunk crowd pushed us down
if I hadn't gone for a walk

while the window was unlocked—
I count it a blessing.

Like that day I booked the wrong airport
and you, without hesitation, picked me up.

The days it could have been
are catalogued in my mind.

Tomorrow's as unreadable as now.
What was perceived as disaster wears

a patinated glaze of grace
like seeing your reflection at the bottom

of a glistening cup you drank from.
How else to explain that if

we didn't see it coming,
it was there all along—probably

there in the doldrum hum of the fridge,
and the train's faulty engine throttle,

there in the garbled murmurs of passengers,
in the falling quiet of snow.

Primary Source

A teacher of mine once said every writer
has only four or five subjects.

There's happiness in repetition
if you don't hear the seconds ticking.

What's worse? Dedicating yourself
to failure or denying it again and again?

Pacher's pupil, a Renaissance carver, perfected
the pine folds of Saint Margaret's robes

using a large axe, then
several smaller ones, then

sanded and painted her in fine detail.
Did he ever think where did the time go?

She stands at the back of a church in Tyrol,
a dragon writhing under her feet.

What do you live for? The quiet
before sunrise or the moments after.

The baby coos in her pram.
I've always wanted to use the word *pram*

at least once in a poem.
Now that I'm a mother,

I've a better understanding of terror
and the miraculous.

Who will she be when she's grown?
Do I have time to shower?

If, as a famous writer decreed, it takes 10,000 hours
to achieve mastery,

I've perfected rocking my hips from side to side,
changing a diaper in dim dawn light.

My baby practices sitting up even in her sleep—
her head bobs like a buoy, her eyelids shudder.

My teacher said sometimes your first line
is your last line.

What's more? The moment she walks
or the moment she falls down.

Looking again at the photo, the dragon
lies curled at Margaret's feet.

I'm holding an image of an image
someone else carved in my hands.

She loves it when I sprinkle my fingers
down on her like rain.

I'm holding the rain in my hands,
and in my hands, the rain holds her.

Demeter's Remorse

All the days, she was mine
alone. That second before
a cut bleeds clean

through a white bandage
red. That summer, we canned
pears. I still haven't opened them.

Dancing in a Dark Room

The music box in my childhood
bedroom without its turnkey,
flecked with gold maple leaves.

Inside, its revolving pins, a song
recorded on the tuned teeth

of a steel comb.

And just an hour ago—
my baby's hot milk breath on my cheek
as she screamed in my ear.

That fleeting thought *it might go on
like this forever*, dancing in a dark room.

And if it did? This grand exercise in denial,
I embrace you. The way my neighbor planted mums

in a tree stump.

The way I scratched my initials
in a trunk and drew a heart around them

with a plus sign.

And my daughter—arms outstretched
on the kitchen floor as she learns
we can walk away from each other.

Honey I won't—
            be gone long.

*

As in a fairy tale, she stows away
with comb and mirror

and runs on stubby legs, laughing
into a grove of trees—

one hair's length away from my reach.

The screen door snapping shut.
And the key? Didn't I have it once?

Hemingway's Homes

Hemingway lived nine years in the house in Key West
now overrun with tourists and polydactyl cats. The last time I was there
I was with Abuela and my mother, the only memory I have of the three of us.
We drove from Miami. Abuela was in her late eighties and Abuelo had died
years before from a final stroke. She was alone much of the time
and quieter, patiently waiting or distracted, I couldn't tell which.
I remember her sitting on the passenger side, staring out the window,
holding the cardboard flap from a gift box above her head to block the darting sun.

Hemingway lived with his second wife Pauline in that house
though he spent much of the time away covering the Spanish Civil War,
which left Pauline alone to oversee the remodeling of the abandoned stately colonial.
He is said to have told her when she built the flagstone patio and dug ten feet deep
into solid coral for the pool, "Pauline, you've spent all but my last penny,
so you might as well have that!" And no one knows for sure if he really said that,
so much surrounding Papa is legend, but there's a penny embedded
in cement at the northernmost end of the pool, a sort of proof, I saw, for the story.

It was for my sake we went to Papa's house. I was nineteen or twenty,
had only read *A Moveable Feast* then, and was completely taken with the idea
that you could live with all your closest writer friends in Paris. Magical
that you could hobnob with Pound, Fitzgerald, and Stein at cocktail parties.
For her part, Abuela hardly paid attention during the tour. She lagged behind the group,
fingering the upholstered chairs (which you could still touch then) and Pauline's
seventeenth-century Spanish Circassian walnut chest, and lifting glances upward
at the many crystal chandeliers, enormous and catching the light—they could have been the same

chandeliers I'll never see, but she had in her home outside Havana where Hemingway also had a home,
Finca Vigía, which he moved to in 1940 with his fourth wife, Mary, using the place in Key West
like a hotel on trips back and forth to Ketchum until he died there in 1961,
a year after my family left Cuba, a year after it was clear the Revolution meant to evict
the wealthy, the middle classes, suspend elections—the Finca, now a government museum.
Perhaps Papa would've chosen to stay in Cuba, like my family, if he hadn't left to get treatment for depression.
Perhaps later, he wouldn't have shot himself. Either way, none of them would return.
My mother was nine years old then, an equal span of time lapsed in a childhood, a marriage, the same

that Hemingway lived in this house with Pauline who stayed on, raised their two boys.
I was in the gift shop, combing the bookshelves, delving into *A Farewell to Arms*, oblivious
to where my mother and Abuela were. The novel Papa finished writing there
I learned from the tour and I could say more about, but then I'd just be repeating the pattern
of moving unexpectedly away. When my mother approached and said, "Abuela met him,"
that he came to a cocktail party hosted at their home I'll never visit with a pool and a palm-lined terrace,
I searched Abuela's face fixed on his photograph and said nothing. She told me she remembered his face,
his moustache, remembered he drank, remembered that Abuelo said he was a great American writer.

But that was all she recalled and all I've remembered. Afterward we drove a half-mile to the southernmost tip
of the continental US with its potbellied monument, a hulking concrete upside-down thimble,
in actuality an old sewer junction that was too heavy to move so they painted like a buoy,
flocked to by visitors and gulls alike. Cuba lies ninety miles away, give or take,
a floating mirage in a humid haze, cresting and collapsing with the waves.
I remember Abuela's eyes anchored on the horizon as she inched closer to the precipice,
as she said *this is the closest we'll get to home* to no one in particular,
as if the wind and the water had a face, had a name before they took her voice away.

II. ANIMAL

Nothing is born unique, to grow up, by itself, alone,
Without a species, but as one of a number of its kind.
— Lucretius, II. 1078-9

Endling

There's a man who cares
for the last snail of its kind,

Achatinella apexfulva, knows precisely
how much moisture, shade, and light

it needs to thrive while it spends
its dwindling time in a glass cabinet.

Don't think about what you can start,
think about what you can end was the advice

I heard on a time management podcast
while slicing bananas

for my daughter's breakfast.
The banana comes from Guatemala

where its kind is plagued
by the *Fusarium* fungus to a possible

almost certain if-it-continues
at-this-rate extinction.

I've never been to Guatemala,
seen a rotting banana plant, or touched

a snail's glossy shell of the kind
that resembles the palette

of a chocolate box—dark brown, chestnut,
white, the occasional splash of mint.

I watch my daughter collect stones
in her plastic bucket, clinking them beside her

as she runs smiling from one corner
of our yard to another—impossible to say

if this July is the warmest month
since the last warmest month,

until it is. My dread, a garden
crawling with invasive insects.

Later, she smashes bananas at the table
between her dirt-crusted fingernails,

laughs at the stickiness while I try to finish
the article I started days ago

about *Achatinella apexfulva,*
whose largest threat is

(you might've guessed) another snail,
Euglandina rosea, aptly named

for its rosy-hued carapace, who will follow
the slimy trail of its gastropod cousin

then yank it from its shell with its serrated tongue
and swallow it like Cronus, shell and all.

When a species is the last of its kind,
it's called an *endling,* a word

that reminds me of *changeling,*
such a fairy-swapped child

I've called my own. I've made
this place for her: warm, soft,

a place that someday I'll not
be allowed to enter,

that may not even survive me.

Fish (in) Tanks

The fish swim in tanks at a restaurant, the doctor's office, or the pet store. We are told we are highly social creatures, mostly kind, but half-truths, like the lone neon fish I watch circle a scaled-down shipwreck, are also half-lies. Air bubbles and tiny jets of water pulse and rise. Out of the side of a bulbous eye, one can see one's watery reflection, all multicolored scales, metallic shades. Sometimes the fish swim together in schools; sometimes they lurk alone underneath plastic arches, swaying green canopies of seaweed, faux phosphorescent castles, rocks, or the bucket seats of miniature Ferris wheels. It is never completely dark as it is in the seabed for which they likely have no nostalgia. Here there are no predators except themselves. Sometimes a fish is nipped to shreds; sometimes others gently bump a lilting body like a buoy to surface. Occasionally they hear the sound of objects hitting glass—a finger, a tail, an open pressed mouth or palm, but every day without fail, food flakes float down. In their shared temperate cubic space, they do not think of themselves as distraction, as backdrop, decor for the world going on outside their own. They just keep swimming towards the glass—the walls and each other—they've learned to live with.

Last Chance to See

It's not easy to watch my decisions grow unfettered.
Once she was a wet animal gently scratching the insides
of my abdomen, letting me know my body wasn't mine alone.

I was permitted to use it for a time, mostly assured
that the animals I bedded down with on this earth
would be there in the morning, roaming in their packs and herds,

digging up the bones of other creatures
as one day my own, though I hardly ever acknowledge
this matter except in the nest of a poem.

With my daughter toddling yesterday, we plunged
our rain boots into piles of wet-slick, colorful leaves.
I didn't used to mind a warm fall day. I enjoyed a hard rain

from a distance. I didn't used to question water,
bees, ice caps, migratory patterns of birds in late winters,
miss the shade of a tree when passing by its stump.

And how can I not question the collective potential
of our species after birthing bombs, automatic weapons,
plastics, and Styrofoam, but also the smallpox vaccine,

lightbulbs, the regenerative patchwork of the ozone layer?
I didn't used to be an insomniac. I didn't used to hear my body say
feel this—*this loss*. I'd just pull it along, a toy on a string.

Loss which comes from the Middle English *los* "ruin, destruction"
and which now carries the additional meaning of failure to keep
what was in one's possession. Someday, someone, maybe me

will tell her about the coral reefs, perennially snowcapped
Everest, an abundance of strawberries year-round. But now I lick
my molting fur, gnaw anxiously on bones, and scrape the crystallized bits

of honeycomb with my teeth. How can I not eye the shallow stream
with its tiny silver fish floating belly up without suspicion?
She points, and I say *They're sleeping. Let's not throw rocks today.*

To her, I can repair anything. That stuck zipper she can't pull,
sealed cup she can't open, wonky eyeball hanging from her bear's plush face.
Mender, healer, fixer: more god than human than animal is a mother

but my body too has grown soft, stretched and looser
in places where it was once hard and muscular, the minerals and immunity
she extracted from me, joints she slackened, throbbing veins she surfaced

to skin, scar left above my pubic bone. Somewhere in those depths,
I know what it means to be animal: to growl, to buck, to claw
against dangers, to love more savagely when threatened to lose.

Demeter's Wager

At first, it didn't seem horrific.
The earth dying as I felt
(if I could) like dying.

I stopped eating, dressing,
coloring my hair. Then I grew sick

of the trees—the way they, full
and green, mocked how I felt,
so I stripped them bare.

After that, it was easier to let go.
Slowly, I gave away
my belongings and hers:

shoes, belts, coats
(still wearing her scent),
books with their dog-eared pages.

Then meadows, estuaries, streams,
forests and their forest creatures—
whole species of birds and fish.

It was almost eerie how light I felt
when I didn't care for earth.

Every day, no surprise—
the sky the color of lint.

When I thought finally
there's nothing left
to save or throw away—

I remembered
I had all eternity,
an empty glass to fill.

I couldn't shrink it
so I expanded it:

the way a bruise on a fruit
rots it entirely.

At some point, we're all deceived.
Some days I hear her voice
in the kitchen, other days

only my echo. Call it grief
or despair—it doesn't matter;
every day I kneel down and feed it.

Bless this rash of fires, this flooded city,
this cracked, parched earth,

so all the water, all the salt,
all the spoils of this world

hear me say: I am your daughter too.

Body, a Field

And when somebody leaves a body as all
must leave some body some time,
we'll say we saw it coming, it happens
so naturally sometimes so we prepare

ourselves to let go of that body of hers
gone slack like our mouths, rubbery
and utterly spent: the utility of words used
and useless to us or anybody else, not useful

certainly for her or her husband or her children
who are sitting next to the space her body kept,
collecting themselves while recollecting her—
and beside them, the porcelain vases hold

their pink peonies, her favorite flower, fully
bloomed in mid-December, their fragrance faint,
extending far back to us in the pews, and where
now I remember the trace of her perfume.

Field, a Body

Flooded with purple chicory and foxgloves
in tall rows of burr-sticking grasses

where rotten brambles of berries, cracked
shells stolen from hawk's nests

and bones from another creature's child
sink, as one day mine. But for now ablaze

in life, in late August, still budding, daring
to turn shades of dark crimson as grass tips yellow.

In death, St. Cecilia's body defied decay,
her soft tortured flesh, a pressed calla lily petal.

Splotched inkdrops mar the page beneath my hand,
blossoms of blue lupine. One day you'll write me.

Abuelo Mío

Abuelo, there are moments when you're in my head,
in evenings sometimes, my whole head, yours.

I wonder how far you travel on these nights between us
stacked like rows of sugar cane stalks, wild, uneven,

quietly ripening in their sheaths in fields far
from your city, old Havana, your dream city and mine.

El ciudad, I've never been to but have scanned
with my black pelican eye. I trace the narrow arm

of Calle Obispo, a vein packed with peddlers hocking
wares and vendors selling papayas next to a polished slew

of Pontiacs, Buicks, and Fords still there, still parked on the side.
I've walked the long esplanade of the Malecón,

its generous wide berth of roadway and seawall
and looked out onto the horizon for you there,

but heard instead whispering lenguas of wind sluicing
the sound of what you tell me in green lapping waves.

What you must've heard on your way home,
the same birds: pelicans, pigeons, gulls.

What you must've seen on facades
of buildings: escuelas, iglesias, cemetarios.

What you must've felt while standing in the same rain
in the same streets of your plaza, bloodied and sweet,

lighting your gray gaze. How it made you flee this city,
this dream city, and love it from a distance.

Abuelo, I hear you and everywhere I try to read you
in faces of birds and your favorite gardenia blooms,

your knuckle-wrinkles and high-ridged thumbnails,
a half-moon shape vaulting at their base.

To touch your hand with my own hand:
the same moons, ridges, and veins.

You're over a hundred now. You must be so tired.
Help me understand what I see when I see you now.

Let me not mistake you for shadow or crow.
Don't let me pass you on the street

and not know that I belong to you. Wear your face
and your body for me, sing to me slow.

American Robin

At first I didn't know it had a name
except to say *bird* and to know the difference

from *human*. Mostly, it's that I can't fly—
can't make a nest with my mouth

from twigs, feathers, paper—
dead leaves, coarse grasses are just that to me.

I can't even begin to smear it all with mud to shape
an oval, or to offer up blue eggs, then wait.

Above, she's perched on a telephone wire,
some worm or grub squirming from her beak,

her young balanced in a nest resting on the cornice
of my porch—three little necks stretch up,

three heads bob down, then up,
soft beaks open—such trust, unshakeable

belief in a world reduced to a blur
of orange breast coming and going

where only one song carries a melody
worth listening for and to think of anything more

than this sensation and shade is inconceivable,
the broken light refracted through the leaves,

and the leaves breaking with the wind
touching them without touch.

Everything's of purpose, divine,
as in the middle of a bud

where a name is called and blooms,
destined to bring forth the flower

or the bird, and I can't even explain why
I'm watching her feed her young—

her offering, their taking, again and again
from one open mouth to another.

III. WORD

Words contain identical sets of letters, but we may claim
That as a general rule, all words cannot be spelled the same;
Thus many other objects may share elements in common,
And yet they may be held to differ in composition.
— Lucretius, II. 693-6

Pupusas at St. Camillus Church, Maryland

Some of us have been singing hymns this hour
while thumbing through the hymnal's worn pages
because we like its weightiness in our palms,
while others have been staring at colored
tracks of carpet threads worn thin and patches
of light slanting in from tinted windows;
and while some of us have been bowing our heads
and bending down on the frayed kneelers,
others have been mouthing the words by rote,
not missing a response or sign of the cross,
and still some of us have been distracted
by the squirming baby in the first pew,
whose timed screams in every silent space
of Mass have been impeccably precise.

We file out of the church into the rain,
where under a taut blue tarp, Salvadoran
women stand selling steaming pupusas
and sliced mangoes in plastic Ziploc bags
as they do every Sunday, even when
I'm not there, which is most Sundays
as they carry out this ritual, having started
the night before, preparing thick Maseca,
then mashing it to flatness and filling it
with queso, frijoles, or chicharron—
the five of them gathered in a kitchen,
laughing, or each in their separate homes
because they are duty bound to go
to church this morning like the rest of us.

They seal pupusas in Tupperware containers,
portable tabernacles, and set aside extras
on dinner plates for children and husbands,
the same men I might pass during the week
as I drive to work—men standing in parking
lot after parking lot waiting for jobs
many of us haven't done, wouldn't do,
and may never, not for that money.
And because they're up that early anyway,
they've helped load the van as their wives
drink café con leche from Styrofoam cups,
getting ready for us to file out of church,
praying the cold rain will bring a generous
crowd since we might have little else to do.

And as one of them deftly slices a mango
this morning, juice spilling onto her fingers,
another attends to the low blue flames
of Bunsen burners, and another ties white
apron cords 'round her friend, and still another
raises a sign: "$2 pupusas, $1 mangoes."
Though I tell myself I'm not hungry, spiced
scents convince otherwise. And as I pretend
I can't wait, I know that really I'm afraid
of the moment I reach the front of the line:
if I speak Spanish, will she stare in disbelief
at my accent, my paler skin, wonder why I'm here,
though we share this tongue, though we both came
to church unsure we'd get what we came for.

Mi Negrita

When Abuela said these words, she clicked her tongue,
stroked my arm as if brushing off dust, the darkening
hue of summer sun. I gave in to her hip, her kiss,
her stale saltine cracker breath on my cheek. I knew

even then as a child to know that the slightest tone
or shade was to be anything unlike the white skin
for which she was, almost legendarily, named Blanca.
I could trace with my fingers her webbing of veins,

purple and light blue tentacles, as if her fishbelly-white flesh
turned out on itself, but the –ita of the word coddled me
even as it spurned. It was meant to. This was before I knew
and long after she was a beauty queen in Cuba, how her skin

was prized then for its glow—how then can stretch farther back,
back farther than memory, hers or mine, or her own mother's
mother's mother, white landowners from Asturias staying
out of the sun as the Yoruba-speaking Africans they enslaved

cut and cured tobacco in long swaths. How then persists—
even in the present-perfect tense of speech: Abuela has splurged
on skin creams. She has taken out her false teeth. She has walked
holding a red umbrella as a parasol in the supermarket parking lot.

We must have made a pair then: her, decked out in high-heeled shoes,
red nails, and always gold somewhere; me in shorts, flip-flops,
smacking gum, how then she might've been terrified to imagine
her tanned nieta mistaken for something other than not quite white.

English II

But Miss I make good money,
he tells me after we've tallied the days
missed. Enough for his black jeans,
black hoodie, sneakers and the rest
to send back to El Salvador.

You should see me Miss at work sometime.
I don't say I was there last week
at the Asian fusion restaurant where water pipes
down a green glass wall and you can order
dim sum at any time of night. I don't say

I didn't see him while he worked in the back
scrubbing dishes, mopping floors, hefting
economy-sized containers of rice and oils,
spices and cans of sauces, sorting silverware
in bins, taking out the trash. . .

when hours later he should be in my class,
where we're reading *Things Fall Apart*
and when he's there, I'm often at his side
to catch him up, to help him get
at least enough to pass.

My grade. I want to know my grade, Miss.
And I have to tell him he's failing
as his older brother chides him
in English and in Spanish,
he doesn't know I understand both

because I didn't say I understand
nor did I offer to speak in my broken Spanish.
If I'm the white maestra to them,
keeper of test scores, the red pen,
of a kind of knowledge

you can buy your way into,
if you're lucky, if you pass,
I wouldn't deny that truth.
I imagine how it might've been
for my mother when she arrived

in Miami in 1960 from Havana,
the only "Hispanic" in her class
when Abuelo forbade singing
or laughter noting how many were dying
or dead or in prison back home.

It's not the same story;
it is the same story. I go back
and forth in time. I hear Abuelo say
lo más importante son los papeles
and my mother says *speak English outside.*

But my student, not yet a man, sits
in front of me in a country, not yet
his home, a country who doesn't see him
or even me, sometimes, and I wonder
what can he learn that he doesn't know from me.

Who am I to say this book is worth
the clothes on his back, the money home?
How can I tell him what a day is worth?
The next morning, his empty chair, and later
Miss, I'm sorry about class.

Blur I

1) to obscure or sully something or someone by smearing or with a smeary substance: chalk, ash, recuerde a dark cloud passing over a mountain, rainfall, crumbling plaster of buildings draped in fog, then crumbling fog; 2) to obscure by making confused in form or outline; make indistinct as in seeing double: salt water I over stone, see you the future tense cuando volveremos meaning when we return faraway and near as in never having left/as in there is nothing left to return to but where are you now? ; 3) to dim the perception or visibility of what you couldn't take embers in ashtrays, crystal goblets emptied of drinks; you hid make dull or insensible as in I can see shallow waters receding my home, the horizon your face; 4) to become indistinct as to blend in, to bleed submerge, white cloud; 5) to make blurs, the trappings of memory, history, tus niños, sus niños: foreign tongues, who can tell nuestra historia, recuérda; 6) a smudge or smear that obscures as if a dream you will not wake from write me this

Blur II

1) to obscure or sully something or **someone** by smearing or with a smeary substance: chalk, ash, **recuerde** a dark cloud passing over a mountain, rainfall, crumbling plaster of buildings draped in fog, then crumbling fog; 2) to obscure by making confused in form or outline; make indistinct as in seeing double: salt water **I** over stone, **see you** the future tense cuando volveremos meaning when we return **faraway and near** as in never having left/as in there is nothing left to return to **but where are you now?** ; 3) to dim the perception or visibility of **what you couldn't take** embers in ashtrays, crystal goblets emptied of drinks; **you hid** make dull or insensible as in **I can see** shallow waters receding **my home,** the horizon **your face**; 4) to become indistinct as to blend in, to **bleed** submerge, **white** cloud; 5) to make blurs, the trappings of memory, history, **tus niños, sus niños:** foreign tongues, who can tell **nuestra historia, recuérda**; 6) a smudge or smear that obscures as if a dream you will not wake from **write me** this

Ethnic Arithmetic

again I check ethnicity boxes

as if I could measure with a stick figure

to derive the crude dimensions I'd wanted

to keep separate as black beans and rice

write fractions ½ and ½ next to squares

a type of equation devise an algorithm

of my identity—those parts

moros y cristianos nunca congri

never together

my mother sighing *it's how a true Cuban eats them*

her quick smile betraying

some part of me quiet another confused as though

like her with a doll and suitcase forever in hand

but *you don't have any accent*

who am I to know who I am

sliding back and forth invisibly

and because of this and maybe only this

she rubs the white of her forearm with two fingers

a gesture I've learned conveys superiority

that says look at me I belong

here not there check guilt shame denial

check every cliché

which feature to cover or show

as if a distinctive mark

a curl of tongue a darker jaundiced eye

check what's fair—what's not

I know exists to erase me

Dear Shame, Dear Sludge

Without you, I'm a pear
in syrup, halved and limp—

your gelatin congealing to my gelasin.
What am I but a Jell-O mold to you,

my jiggler, my juggernaut? I've a compulsion
to move, but when I think I think for myself,

I'm stuck with you, fly on my paper.
Sometimes I've misplaced you,

but like a sock, you turn up at the bottom
of the drawer. You're always there—

pebble in my shoe. Shoo fly, don't bother.
I've tried to lose you. Sound batty?

How you've gaggled me, baffled me
with thyme and ruse. If this is a game,

I'd rather zigzag, hem haw, pass.
I've lost track of the thread again,

so sew up the hole. I'm sensitive.
I'm rosy, a pocketful of posey.

I've got laundry. I get lonely. Chuck me
an ace, throw me a stone, darling, your lack

of conversation is hardly feckless.
I beg of you, keep your distance—

no, come closer. My promiscuity
with mediocrity is by no means reflexive

of you, subject and object of myself.
I could never be unfaithful,

harlot though I've tried to be.
Transgress? Sure, I've wanted to, so sue me.

I've never done what you didn't think to do, too.
We're yoked like oxen to the plow

so let's keep digging rotted potatoes.
It's hard work to keep them from the worms.

No kidding. This is fun. I'd like to start
the day with you again. Hear

how I call for you underneath
my sloughed speech.

So many tulips in the shed. I've got
news for you, cards I've not written yet.

Want not, waste not. It's all roots.
Fertile soil is the filthiest. I've no

regrets spending my time with you,
chronic pneumonia to my pneuma.

When I say there's no cure for this penumbra,
what I mean is *Come back, I miss you.*

After Viewing Cassatt's Little Girl in a Blue Armchair *without My Ex*

You should've been there
at the Degas-Cassatt exhibit.
You would've hated it. There I was,
peering between gawking heads
(ones you would've towered over)
when that iridescent blue,
a robin eggshell blue drew me close.
It was not the girl reclining limply
in the massive armchair, so large
her feet dangled above ground.
It was not the scrappy dog sitting
beside her, but upon seeing them both,
I wanted to sit in that big blue chair too
with its multicolored brushstrokes
resembling a pattern not quite distinguishable,
but vaguely familiar like something
from a grandmother's house, but maybe
in Paris in 1879, haute couture.

You should've been there; I'm certain
you would've hated it. Bored like the girl.
Degas even brought the girl, a child of his friend's,
to sit for Cassatt, slumped, not dainty or proper.
Don't you wish you could've been there—
I mean, when they were painting?
They were never lovers, Degas and Cassatt,
but their art, I learned, grew in concert with each other.
He dabbled in her metallic paints; she experimented
with his printmaking, colored frames.
Evident also is Degas's hand in the corner
of the room beyond the chairs—quick, sharp
signature strokes of grayish, silvery brown paint
not found elsewhere, but certainly, his.

What did Cassatt think of it?
And though it's hardly the same at all,
I recall that mosaic pencil holder I made
(the one you said was a fourth grade art project)
and how I did it wrong, the flat shiny glass
should've been facing the front, *the rough backside*
should cling to the grout you said, so that now
there are three craggy sides and one smooth face.

What did Cassatt think of it?
She, who then repositioned the armchair,
reworking it to align to the now sloping wall,
shifting the squirrely-haired dog to the floor
then back again, doubting herself,
and probably always while looking at her painting
knowing that the gray-brown corner was not done
by her hand, however pleasing to the eye.
Surely she felt something about it
even if they were not lovers. Later, Degas
was quoted as saying *I don't admit a woman
draws that well,* a kind of backhanded compliment
(even she recognized) about her work.
O you should've been there.
You wouldn't have even noticed the dog.

Cherchez la Femme

(from French meaning "find the woman")

There never was the hysterical woman
locked in an attic, an animal on all fours
tearing out her hair or threading a loom
and unthreading it every night so she'd never
have to bed her believed-to-be-dead husband's friends.
There never was the angry woman wailing
over a kitchen sink rubbing her hands raw
trying to cleanse herself of death or a group
of women banded together denying men sex
as if they weren't already assumed plundered.
There never was a black or red dress,
a smoking gun, la femme fatale, *cherchez la femme!*
There never was a willing muse. Never a bruise,
a blemish, a scar. There never was the woman
sacrificed on an altar with goats to sanctify a city
who thought she had it coming and they,
they would be saved. There never was the woman
who drowned herself inexplicably in a lake as if
there was no cause for her nightmares. Never
the scarlet A, the prison break, the abortion clinic bust,
a mob wielding pitchforks, the missed rent,
stolen paycheck, burning pyres, the chant
of *lock her up!* There never was that tower
with a key, long strands of braided hair she could cut
herself free from. There was the walk home,
and every day the gauntlet of howlers, hollers,
hoopla, the construction worker whistles,
the *can I get some fries with that shake,*
daddy's girl, teacher's pet, stank liquor breath,
unmerciful panic, unheard prayer. The silence
after a thousand doors slammed shut. *Slut!*
There was a blunt instrument. Her body.
There was an accident. Her mouth.
There never was the hysterical woman.
There was the man and his myth, and they would not die
no matter how many times we cried father.
No matter how many times they were swallowed
in dirt, the earth just spit them back out.

IV. EARTH

Certain things arise from only a certain kind of mother. . . .
Each species rises from specific seeds,
Each thing springs from the source that has the matter that it needs,
The primary particles, and comes into the boundaries
Of light.
— Lucretius, I. 168-171

Little Shadow

Impossible to conceive of the never
                    having-been-me without you.

Would she walk brazenly in stilettos?
                    She'd be well rested, for sure.

Would she ever find cheerios in her bra?
                    Then eat them?

Would she have published a novel by now?
                    Has anyone read it?

Spine straighter? Breasts, the same size?
                    Her back and feet, less sore?

Would she wonder all day, entirely
                    hers, what am I missing?

*

One day, you were invisible.
          The next, you were invisible
                    to everyone but me.

You were inside my body
          while I was outside;
                    outside was everything else.

*

I wrote to a friend you are my little shadow
the way you follow me throughout the house,
but could I have written you are the shadow of me?
The way you crinkle the nose we share or clasp
our hands together. Shadow-like.

*

In the delivery room, had it gone as planned,

I would have pushed and you would have been pulled,

but in our case, I was cut and you were lifted out.

Does process matter? Having never-been-a-you before

having never-been-a-me, who was delivered and when?

*

I look back on what I'd written before
                like someone peering over my shoulder

wearing a heavy floral scent. I say
                it's done because I want nothing more,

can't conceive of it. I may never write
                a poem without you in it.

*

From the Latin prefix *con*—"together"

                and the root *capere*—"to take"

conceive suggests "to take together" or to pair.

                As defined in the *OED*, conceive:

                1) create an embryo by fertilizing an egg; or

2) form or devise (a plan or idea) in mind.

                She was conceived, and for a time, we had no idea.

                        I conceived of her birth before her birth

to prepare myself. I gave little thought to after. I had no plan,

                no conception of her or me.

*

Each day, this spring
                seeking flowers
you pick dandelions
                and I let you

crumple them

        in your fist. Yellow dust.

Flawvers!

        Yes, they're yellow.

Flawvers!

        Yes, we can pick them.

Flawvers!

        All gone!

*

You wandered in like a page blown
by the wind, conceived and delivered.
One day you may write to me.

*

She plucks off plastic electrical outlet covers

like petals or the way I might finger the still

red-gold curls of her hair that smells like wheat

and strawberries. She would like to plug in:

dandelion heads, the tip of my pen, a crayon.

When I'm reading, she sometimes sits next to me,

reading, and sometimes, she shuts my book.

I'm reading. Mama reading. Does the first

or third person matter? Having never-been-a-she,

before having never-been-a-you? *Mama I reading*, she says.

*

You want more? *Nod.* Cheese or apple?
        Cheeese. What do you say? *Pleeese.*

She flicks her fingers under her chin,
        the sign I incorrectly taught her

for please which really means thank you
        and elsewhere means fuck off.

*

Learning to walk on the grass, she stumbles
over her feet, then crawls over to me,
clings to my legs *Pick me! Pick up!*

After Viewing Cassatt's The Oval Mirror with My Daughter Sleeping Next to Me

The boy looks away
while resting his cheek on hers
smiling at a thought.

Not holding him tightly, the mother
smiles at the thought
of his thought

—or, he's smiling
at her thought
or the thought of her.

O the possibilities
of objects and desires
waiting to be named

[ball, book, shoes,
shoelaces, keys, remote control,
mechanical or real puppy]

—my own daughter
demanding more of myself
to fill desires she doesn't

have words for yet
[but boy she can bark!]
like *hunger* or *loneliness*

needs I can only soothe
like the toothaches
I numb by distraction,

cool gummy toys, my nipple.
I see how dangerous
the mirror is behind them

like a halo recalling the Madonna
and child, impossibly
embodied selflessness.

When Degas quipped to Cassatt
"it has all your qualities
and all your faults,"

he didn't know
how right he was
about mothers.

O the possibilities
of the lips
that form a hole

to make desire
first a sound, then
a word—

how it knows nothing
about surrendering.
Just ask the child.

Letter to Another Mother with Excerpts from the Handbook on Mothering

which no one receives anymore
but by which we're conditioned
to believe exists
and without which
we're damn near harmful
to our children
where it might read
on p. 1087: *to soothe*
swollen neck glands, dip
buttered toast in warm milk,
watch the yellow globules
float to the top of the milkskin,
which even as an image
I find comforting to imagine,
but what can I tell you
about the blank page
under the entry
active shooter drill?
Where would I start?

I guess with guns,
guns in schools,
in churches, in Walmarts
next to backpacks
and hermetically sealed
organic babyfood pouches.
I guess with bulletproof
vests, security guards,
checkpoints, lockdown
drills, 9-1-1 calls to parents
from closets saying maybe
their last goodbyes?
I guess this wouldn't be
a standard entry, a typical
poem, a normal time.
Do you remember when
that was? Last week
I learned to knit a scarf
and then a hat, it seems
like something mothers do.
I canvassed, wrote thank you
cards for my daughter's
second birthday, and to Dr. Blasey Ford.

Knitting helps
pass time,
even dark times,
gives my hands something
to do—and they want,
desperately
something to do. Hands
that did swaddle an infant,
offer a finger to suck,
but can't protect her
from the haze of hate
and fear which governs
every breath in the present.
Hands that want
to be useful, beloved, worthy.
Now my daughter won't
wear any other hat—
I guess you could say
I feel kind of proud
like I did that
I made that hat
I made that child
having carried that body
inside my body, then watched
that extension of myself
drift away
like a future
I'll never see—
a rain shower happening
in a desert, a spoon
dipped into a cloudy bowl
of chicken noodle soup
made by an artificially
intelligent machine.
P. 440: *To clear a stuffy nose:*
boil a broth from leftover
carcasses, necks, livers,
add chopped vegetables.
Simmer and strain.
There's something about seeing
your future in front of you,
quite plainly stumbling
over rocks, tree stumps,
getting tangled up in socks,
and knowing you've failed it

before it ever had a chance.

I've done some good
things too though. Don't you
wish trying was enough,
as we tell our children it is?
I've purchased BPA-free plastics,
checked for parabens, phthalates,
pesticides. Prepared her
body with the prescribed
amount of vaccines—thin
but essential protections
against diseases, pestilences,
but no, it's not a shield
for bullets, a boat for rising
sea levels, it won't prevent
raging wildfires, droughts,
food shortages. I no longer
seek perfection or expect
to do any better collectively
than our ancestral empires.
There's something about sleeping
in these times. I don't
do it well. Do you?
What's your trick?
There's something about feeling
glad or talking about trees,
weather, what kind of fruit
pie to bring to the neighbor's
potluck? Especially if I want
to be thought of as thoughtful,
considerate of potential allergens,
the harm I've already
caused inadvertently,
but nonetheless have caused.
I've sought to make amends
but it's like patching a hole
in the knee-space
of her jeans, gluing a wheel
to a toy truck, knowing full well
it won't spin again.

I'm often told to save
things: her first lock
of hair, baptismal dress,

first drawing with crayons,
first drawing with watercolors,
a video of her first word
ball or *book,* first sentence
Take that away or *Here you go*
Mama. You know p. 878
create a scrapbook in spare time,
tuck keepsakes away
in a box tied with a ribbon.
But how to stow away
clean air, a cool breeze?
Whales, green trees,
ice cream—these things.
These things, how do we
save them? And if we could have,
what do we say when we're asked
why we didn't?

Student Handbook

A is for alligator and AR-15.
B is for backpack, bumpstock, bolt—
what you lock or run from.
C is for closet, where the teacher tells you to hide.
D is for duck.
E is for everybody hold hands as we exit the building.
F is for four or five friends eating lunch.
G is for gum and guns, which are not allowed at school, *of course*.
H is for house or H could be for help.
I is for "I can" statements as in I can draw, I can dance,
I can hear shots—"at first I heard a pop
and thought it was a bag because people do that."
J is for jiggle like Jell-O: the handles
of a locked classroom door, the hands of a teacher.
K is for her keys jingling in a kindergarten classroom.
L is for lockdown.
M is for music, maracas, magazines
of thirty rounds on a website "cheaperthandirt."
N is for the NRA buying politicians, and thus schools—
and *how is this normal?* #neveragain
O is for over and over and over again.
P is for play! Pretend to be sleeping polar bears.
Q is for question as in why is it raining,
how are babies made, is this an open carry state?
R is for rules—look both ways
before crossing the street, clean up
your mess, report unhealthy thoughts,
or R is for reading, recess.
S is for school, *obviously*, and scared.
T is for teachers and 238
school shootings since Columbine.
U is for unthinkable, unpatriotic,
United States of America.
V is for vigils.
W is for walkouts, when, where, why.
X is for *in the crosshairs, children.*
Y is for yellow, slow down, and
Z is for zeroing out or in.

Demeter Remembering

I planted seeds where no one thought anything could grow,
an insurance policy for raising her among humankind.
There, in damp caverns or wedged in sand or under sheets of ice,
I buried crocks full of pestilence and greed,
knowing the likelihood of them being unearthed.
And what did it feel like? To kill
my darlings? To kill—
it led me straight to hell
where I knew they'd be waiting.

*

Of course, they blamed a childless woman
for opening the jars. The altar of motherhood
too sanctified. I cut first—or maybe
it was my own daughter running away. Either way,
you know what they say about us—women
or gods, we're a jealous lot.
But mothers? There's no ends to the earth
we wouldn't scorch or drown with love.

*

I had my doubts. We mothers do.

Even if she returned to me,
I knew some part of me would not.

I took the emptiness of my hands
and scattered it everywhere.

Is there another way to be true to yourself?

Forgiveness has never been something
I wanted. As if I had a choice.

What Was to Keep the Tigers at the Zoo

what was to keep the tigers at the zoo
from leaping over the embankment
no chain-link fence no barrier

between one harmless gesture
or one skipping toddler
and a giant crushing claw

I could see this scenario
playing out in front of the frightened
clutching their purses and children

even when my daughter and I
went to the park by our house
to throw stones

into the shallow stream
filled with minnows and twigs
bottlecaps and plastic wrap

I took a step back
to watch her
my foot grazing

a yellowjacket or wasp
we are assured we can endure
almost anything

but I thought while running
in circles flailing my arms
someone would hear me

and break the cycle
of vicious then numbing stings
maybe I've always pictured

a lighthouse scanning
the shores and someone
walking us back inside

as I did with my daughter
where we showered
and I dressed her wounds

with Cookie Monster Band-Aids
hydrocortisone cream and whispered
shh you're OK now humming in her ear

when all I wanted was the same
soft lulling song to sleep
I can no longer start

sentences with all I wanted
we are headed straight toward
a reckoning when we wonder

why the fish have gone
missing why the fires burn
incessantly why the rain

drums on corrugated rooftops
to cover them entirely and who
let the tiger out of its cage

who caged it and who or what
will save us from ourselves I can't
dream of my own private island

an offshore account with elite membership
to the Elon Musk rocket ship club
we are tethered here in sailor knots

wearing flimsy orange safety vests
toting first aid kits caution tape
waving at danger zones

with lighted sticks labeling
the high risks of breathing
while poor or hungry

or having darker skin or speaking
a foreign tongue or carrying obscene
debt or caring for our children

we who invented forgiveness
but do not give it
and would not know now

whom to ask or how
for the good news coming
is we have each other

as well as the bad
while the mornings
are mortal and softly lit

and the majority of us
long for another then
another and our mothers

V. CELESTIAL

Finally, we all arise from seed celestial,
Because the same sky overhead is father of us all.
From him our nurturing mother, Earth…
And that which was sent down to earth from heaven's aethereal shore
Is taken up again into the quarters of the sky.
— Lucretius, II. 991-1001

Why I No Longer Wear My Mother's Ring

In one version, my mother pulls the ring
from the bottom of her dresser drawer:
three thin silver hoops twined
and tells me, *keep it,*

her mother gave it to her;
now she's giving it to me
to pass to my youngest
when the time comes.

Plain when compared
to the rest of the gems displayed
(her deep amethyst pendant, amber
topaz earrings, four green tourmalines,
an opal set on gold spokes):
all this, nearly a lifetime collected.

In another version, she finds
the band at a yard sale.

I've polished it to shine
similar to one she had
but lost—though this is close
to how it looked on her hand,
how it felt—the weight
not even an ounce in mine.

In a more obscure telling,
the ring passed as in the first account
but this time no words spoken
no other stones visible.

I wear it for over twenty years
until a link breaks and it pinches
my skin, snags on sweaters, scarves,
gloves, anything that'll catch.

Unwillingly, I take it off
to have it soldered
but not before I tell her
(my mother) the story

of how I broke it, her gift
and that's when I learn:

She doesn't remember ever having
such a ring, much less giving it.

Here and There a Thing That Glitters

It seemed so otherworldly—
        unmistakable red plumage flitting
from tree to tree industriously
           under a milk-gray sky, had it been
any other day I might've kept walking, hard sometimes
       to say yes to the day, hard to say please with intensity,
          though I mean to, I trace my finger
       upwards as my daughter repeats me like a colorful cartoon
parrot strutting in her puffed coat, mismatched gloves
      woo-pec-aaa, she feels the word thoroughly
         lilt then melt on her tongue as a snowflake,
      another first for her every days of firsts.
She is two and feels the world thoroughly.

My mistake may have always been
      from the start—naming it, believing
a name was the same as knowing, that rush
        of red brushing a bluish sky, knocking open
door after door of memory, my mistake
      I didn't mean to open that, didn't mean
        to break into song, somewhere
      I read Georgia O'Keeffe would hum sounds
of colors she painted, and I wonder how my voice is seen—
      is it pink, blue, indigo? I violet for her—
        is it possible I've come into this world
      just for her to see me in it?
It is all that light and dictions are made of.

Here and there a summer,
      a verb, a thing that glitters
above the tree line in the dead of winter,
        all the bare trees, pale clouds and all I-495
are humming a light blue electromagnetic fuzz,
      this morning's rooster call while I push
        her in a red stroller, she is kicking up
      her legs while a woodpecker drums hole after hole
in a maple tree above us, diligently searching
      for beetle or grub, perfectly nameless useful
        things, what use is memory,
      all those romantic crepuscular skies,
crenellating crocuses sprung, fireflies caught in a jar.

Every ache is called a *boo-boo,*
   to miss her dada or leave
a toy behind, to wake suddenly in the night alone,
    a small nick on her fingertip
demands looking to, especially if there's nothing
   to see, when she has no expression
     for the streams running along her cheeks
  and I remember the first time I cut her
infant toenail too close and it bled for what seemed hours,
   and there are moments now that remind me
     of that mistake, wherever she has no alternative
  way to say she's so sad so adequately enough
as to flail her wingless body like a bird glued to a sidewalk.

I feel an impulse to stand still,
   to take pictures, document,
already I've forgotten most days, what was I like
    as a child? she'll ask. What was I like as a mother?
O there was that world, I'll say, it was blue, and beyond us
   it seemed another world, also blue,
    in the ancient texts there's no word for blue
  so it was believed for a long time they couldn't see
the many things of blue, fish and their fish
   in a blue-green sea, then herons and chicks,
     then brown-blue earthworms, butterflies
  and caterpillars, Siamese cats with their blue-gray eyes, then me,
then you, and by then she'll have forgotten her question.

Everything's an appendage:
   my house, my truck, my woo-pec-aaa
and leaving it necessitates ritual, elocution, a careful
    verbal tiptoe, time for truck to go to sleep
in a bed of Legos, we'll be back, leaving's
   an uneasy feeling, a blue-green feeling,
    a snowflake falling in a sea of white feeling,
   to fall in love with the falling, I think, is the thing,
but not the loss or longing, that's key, yes, if such a key
   is found anywhere, darling—finding it isn't,
    Mama, I remember that one, a book we've read,
   she was such a little thing, a few months then,
as she sits into my legs, soft bird with gangly knees, makes a nest of me.

Nest

It looked like a hairball caught
in the hanging plant, the one we meant

to toss as it was dying or dead already
in late October, leaving us a chill,

but you stopped, noticing the rise and fall
of feathers? *It's breathing,* you said. *Now we can't. . .*

No we can't, I agreed. *How long will it stay?*
I was a spider in the center of its web: knots of waiting.

You were sweeping the porch clear of brown leaves,
pine needles, double-winged samaras from the maple tree.

I'd check on it daily, observing
that by the time I woke, still dark, it was gone—

but by nightfall, returned, a new ritual added
to our mostly dependable evenings:

>   warm the bottle, pee one pink line on a paper strip
>   means not a baby, give a bath, brush her teeth,

>   read a book, sing a song, and then, only after we laid
>   our daughter down, I'd watch from the window its slow pulse:

the white spots on its puffed-out body expand
and contract, bill tucked into its chest, body curled

in sleep not unlike hers when I rose those first few weeks
in the middle of the night to be certain she was still

breathing—strange and suddenly there, my hand
hovering over her, astonished, from the Latin *extonare*:

>   "to thunder, to leave someone shocked with wonder"
>   even after we'd shared a dwelling, my body for nine months.

And the bird, a Carolina wren, would it survive winter?
Live its spring here and bear children, their tiny beaks

stretching ceaselessly for food? I realize how silly
this sounds, but I took a kind of pride

that the bird chose our home as refuge
from the wind and first frosts, the neighborhood cats

prowling suburban yards. And though I knew better,
I shouldn't have gotten so close, my breath frosting the glass,

when I'm certain I surprised it, two heads perked up,
and after a moment, flew. Two, I'd never guessed two.

Will they return? I asked. You shrugged your shoulders,
placed your hand on my back. And this is so me of me

to hear you say not if *it chooses to* but if it chooses *you.*

Use Bottom Cushion for Flotation Device

for C.T.

Truth is probably half the time I say something,
I say something I don't mean to say
or wish I hadn't said or it's nicer than saying
what I'd really like to say like where it reads
bolted on the plane seat in front of us:
"use bottom cushion for flotation device"
as a way of saying "you're screwed,"
and maybe that's too obvious to say,
but imagine if the plane went down over water—
wouldn't it have been nice, lifesaving perhaps,
if someone had said "your seat is a goddam floaty,"
which also implies hope in its utterance
that even on a plane precipitously descending,
you might just survive. Seems better than saying nothing—
a kind of Pascalian wager for language,
for when you've nothing to lose, but words,
a seat cushion, and a hulking metal cage with wings
buttressing a 30,000-foot descent.

True even if it's one of those things you wish
you didn't have to say, but say it anyway
because the one time it's worth saying
might be *this* time, and you've no way
of knowing. It's why the tour guide
at the historic cemetery we visited,
Bonaventure, from where we're flying home
on this plane of good or ill fortune,
told us not to trample over the graves,
to keep our voices low and walk respectfully
between mowed rows of grass: line after line
of mouths filled with dirt, because somebody
once danced on Johnny Mercer's grave
and someone else spat on their ancestor
and it might be said they'd both been waiting
all their lives to do those things—
it wouldn't have mattered what the tour guide said
or didn't say moved as they were to act without words.

There are so many ways to say "I love you"
in this world: side-by-side burial plots,
shared sticks of gum, picnics by the sea.
There are so many ways to say "I'm sorry":
side-by-side burial plots, shared sticks of gum,
picnics by the pond. I feel there's an infinite number

of lines I've crossed out for you,
but that's not true—just once I'd like to say
something I mean not like I mean it.
I used to think the absence of suffering was happiness.
I used to think happiness was finding
something or someone you loved so much
you'd do it over and over again, but now I think
that's a kind of unsustainable masochism,
which isn't what I meant to say exactly.
The way I feel about you has nothing to do
with planes or picnics or burial plots. It has nothing to do.
It's like a puppy chasing its tail. It's why I don't sleep

well if you're not lying next to me. It's why
"in the event of decompression," there's nowhere
I'd rather be than with you by my side. I'd like you
to know "in the event of a water landing,
an oxygen mask will appear in front of you,"
and I'll be that person who'll help you put it on—
I may even be that person who'll forget
to put it on herself first, the kind of person
the announcement was written for. The kind of person
who's made cloud animals while eyeing the vomit bag.
You're the person I've written this poem for—
the kind of person who doesn't read poetry
or only as an occasional shared indulgence like banana splits.
I don't want an occasion to say that when I'm with you,
I feel like putting coins in the jukebox. When I'm with you,
I'm descending into the deepest part of my life
with a complimentary beverage. I can rest my eyes now.
Know what I mean? We don't have anything to lose.

After the Storm

The coffee-stained, chipped cup
with lipstick on the rim. The urn filled
with ashes from three dead dogs. The handwoven
Turkish rug. The antique lamp. The Father's Day card
scrawled in crayon that bled colorfully. Some

small memory reaching
from storage bins, curios,
the one dry box in the attic—
how surprising

to find it now

as if someone smuggled it out
and it was never meant for that first moment
but for this one,

like the daughter who listens
to her mother's voice
on a VHS tape sing back to her
and rewinds it again.

El Regreso

Under the orange glow of the flamboyan tree,
they talk of el regreso
while sipping espresso from paper demitasses
and at a roundtable after dinner, after dominoes

they will talk of el regreso.
Of old Cuba, of old Havana, of all things old
at a roundtable after dinner, after dominoes
Do you remember the lechón? Do you remember tres leches cake?

Hombre, we never feasted better.
Nodding, the men agree, puff on cigars.
Do you remember how they sent our brothers to be slaughtered on Playa Girón?
They straighten the pleats of their guayaberas, lean into their chairs.

No one starts to leave.
Shall we have another round?
They straighten the pleats of their guayaberas, lean into their chairs.
Plumes of smoke rise from their cigars, resting in ashes.

And the china I hid in the ceiling before we left, do you remember?
Niña, it is there, it is yours—all of it.
Plumes of smoke rise from cigars resting in ashes
under the orange glow of the flamboyan tree.

Persephone Remembering

What need have I of oracles
when I have always had my mother?
My dreams have never been prophesies
in which I kissed her hand
and begged her
to beg me
for forgiveness
as if my immortal life depended upon
hearing her words,
words, I've always believed too much in.

Theory of Probability II

The moon tugs the earth through

      tides and seasons, but it's the earth

I read, that possibly shaped the moon

      into a pockmarked and bulged egg

forming it before it formed. I believe it.

      One day I caught my daughter's face

            at an angle

     as if it were the same

pixilated puffed face first sonically rendered—

      her body forming before formed.

I understood in that moment I understand nothing

      about probability: a question of odds

         suggesting a future

     and its shape, a matter

of how likely or unlikely for debris to churn

      into an oblong ball and cool

or for cells in dark chambers to cross

      over double-helix binds, bloodstreams,

        blighted fields of stars—

what the tide lets in lets out.

NOTES

The section headers are from Lucretius. *De Rerum Natura (The Nature of Things)*. Translated by A. E. Stallings. Penguin Classics, 2007.

The poem "Endling" is inspired by "The Last of Its Kind" by Ed Yong published in *The Atlantic,* July 2019.

"Ethnic Arithmetic" is a contrapuntal poem and meant to be read three ways: the left side, the right side, and together. As in a musical composition, there are two distinct melodies and the third is a compilation of the movement back and forth between the two, resulting in a new harmonic relationship.

The poem "Student Handbook" borrows text from survivor Jonathan Coates, a seventeen-year-old student, who was in the cafeteria at the time when a fifteen-year-old shooter opened fire on the first day of classes at Perry Hall High School in Perry Hall, MD, in 2012. One student was critically wounded and teachers quickly disarmed the shooter, preventing further injuries and casualties. Classes resumed the following day. As of April 2019, there have been 238 school shootings since Columbine according to *The Washington Post.* Though the number of school shootings in the US is now higher, data is updated only periodically, and this number was the most up-to-date at the time of publication.

The poem "After the Storm" was inspired by Manny Fernandez's *The New York Times* article "What They Saved: Texans Reflect on Treasures Plucked from Hurricane Harvey" and *The Daily* podcast, both published on September 5, 2017. When the interviewer on the podcast asked Ms. Kris Ford-Amofa, who returned to her home one week after Harvey, if there was anything she was glad she found, she mentioned the VHS tape of her mother singing at church that was salvaged from the wreckage. It is the only reason she still owned a VCR.

ACKNOWLEDGMENTS

My deepest thanks to the editors of the publications where the following poems were first published, sometimes in different forms:

Another Chicago Magazine: "Demeter's Wager"

Barrow Street: "Theory of Probability I"

Bullets into Bells (online): "Student Handbook"

Copper Nickel: "Ab Ovo"

Hinchas de Poesia: "Abuelo Mío"

Little Patuxent Review: "Cherchez la Femme," Finalist for the 2019 Enoch Pratt Free Library Poetry Contest

Matter: "Ethnic Arithmetic"

PANK: "Endling"

On the Seawall: "Nest"

Poet Lore: "Pupusas at St. Camillus Church, Maryland" and "American Robin"

PALABRA: A Magazine of Chicano and Literary Art: "El Regreso"

Rise Up Review: "After the Storm"

SWWIM: "Primary Source"

The Cortland Review: "Field, a Body"

Some of these poems have been previously published in the chapbook, *Mother Tongue*, by Dancing Girl Press, 2018.

*

I am immensely grateful for all the support and kindness I have received from so many people—family and friends, teachers and mentors. I apologize to anyone I may have inadvertently forgotten here to mention by name. The list is long. They say it takes a village to raise a child, and writers also know it takes a village to bring a book into the world. Know that if you are reading this book, I am grateful to you too.

To Eileen Myles, for selecting this book for publication and seeing its true vision amid so many other wonderful books out there, I thank you.

Thank you to the dedication of Christine Stroud and Mike Good at Autumn House Press. I couldn't be more pleased to be working with you on bringing this book through its final stages out into the world.

With enormous appreciation for the following institutions who have supported me in writing: the University of Maryland, the University of Vermont, the Bread Loaf Writers' Conference, and the National Writing Project.

My utmost thanks to my teachers and mentors for their generosity, support, and belief in my work, especially to the UMD MFA faculty: Michael Collier, Joshua Weiner, Elizabeth Arnold, and Stanley Plumly, whose voice I can still hear sometimes in my head when revising and it makes me smile. To Michael, thank you for your continued guidance and support long after graduation and the first poetry workshop I ever took. To Josh and Gerard Passannante, professor of English and Classics at UMD, it is a testament to the intellectual rigor and capacity for the imagination that Lucretius is embedded in these pages. It is a testament to those seminars where I was privileged to be your student and am still thinking about them years later. To Liz, thank you for your keen eye and ears on the early versions of some of these poems when I was learning how to write them.

To Carol, who first suggested that I "write about it," and every week I brought you a poem for some time thereafter. I can't thank you enough for your steadfast belief in me.

To Sarah Bartlett, thank you for beautifully facilitating the first community of writers I ever joined in *Women Writing for (a) Change*, VT.

To the poets I'm grateful to name among my dearest friends, you are my first readers and confidantes. To Rachel Phillips and Matilda Young—you may have read every poem in this book, and I thank you not only for your insights on revision, but also for the years of friendship that I value above all. To my fellow mother-poets, Chloe Yelena Miller and Julia Kolchinsky Dasbach, who understand the balance (or lack thereof) and have offered some critical attention to poems here. Your strength, words, and care continuously inspire me!

Thank you especially to the talented poets who I've had the privilege of being their student even for a short time: Stephanie Burt, Afaa Michael Weaver, Natasha Trethewey, Karin Gottshall, Sasha West, Jenny George, Jennifer Chang, and Matthew Olzmann. Thank you for your generosity of spirit, insight, guidance, and above all encouragement and community. It's often what kept me going. To Jennifer Grotz and Lauren Francis-Sharma, thank you for all you do to make the Bread Loaf Writers' Conference possible.

To Wyn Cooper, thank you for your believing in the book. Your words were exactly what I needed to hear when I needed to hear it.

To Mikra and Valdete—thank you for providing a refuge to write some days from the "birdhouse" in your backyard, and for the many lively discussions and drinks, sometimes about writing.

To my Boston College familia—Amanda, Darrell, Jen, Laura, Ryan, Siti, Victoria, and Yesenia—there's no group of people I laugh and cry with more than you all of you. You see me and always have.

To my parents, Rosa and Doug, and to my sister, Alexia, thank you for everything.

To Maia and Aidan, so much of you are in these pages. You are my heart.

To my husband, Colin, thank you for everything else I cannot put into words (try as I might). There's nowhere else on the planet I'd rather be than with you.

Sara R. Burnett is also the author of *Mother Tongue*, a poetry chapbook (Dancing Girl Press, 2018), and has published poems and essays in *Barrow Street*, *Copper Nickel*, *Matter*, *PANK*, and elsewhere. A finalist for the 2019 Enoch Pratt Free Library Poetry Contest and recipient of scholarships from the Bread Loaf Writers' Conference, she holds an MFA in Creative Writing from the University of Maryland and an MA in English Literature from the University of Vermont. She lives in Maryland with her husband and children. *Seed Celestial* is her first book.

NEW & FORTHCOMING RELEASES

Seed Celestial by Sara R. Burnett
Winner of the 2021 Autumn House Poetry Prize
selected by Eileen Myles

Bittering the Wound by Jacqui Germain
Winner of the 2021 CAAPP Book Prize
selected by Douglas Kearney

The Running Body by Emily Pifer
Winner of the 2021 Autumn House Nonfiction Prize
selected by Steve Almond

Entry Level by Wendy Wimmer
Winner of the 2021 Autumn House Fiction Prize
selected by Deesha Philyaw

The Scorpion's Question Mark by J. D. Debris
Winner of the 2022 Donald Justice Poetry Prize
selected by Cornelius Eady

Given by Liza Katz Duncan
Winner of the 2022 Rising Writer Prize in Poetry
selected by Donika Kelly

Ishmael Mask by Charles Kell

Origami Dogs by Noley Reid

AUTUMN HOUSE PRESS

For our full catalog please visit: http://www.autumnhouse.org